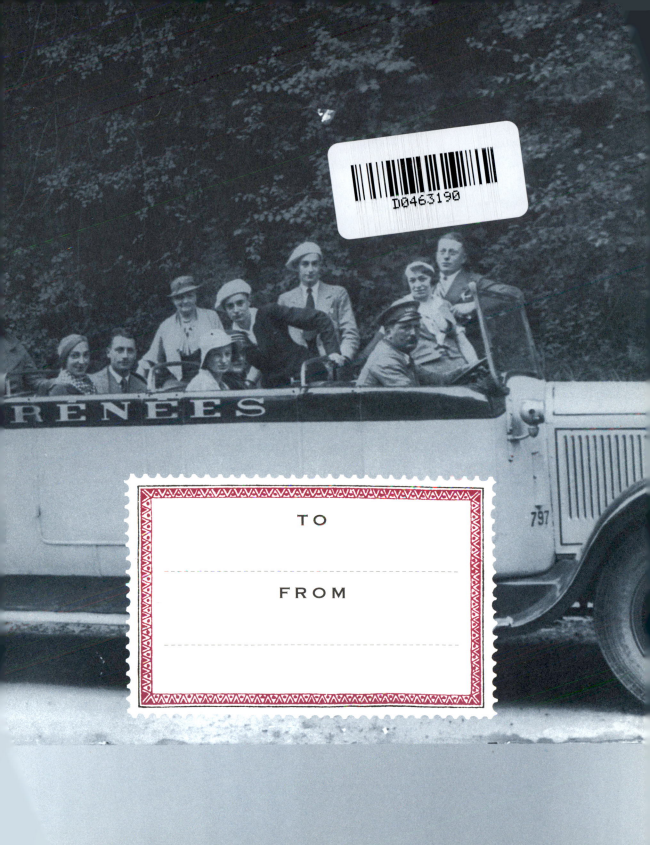

RENEES

797

TO

_____

FROM

_____

_____

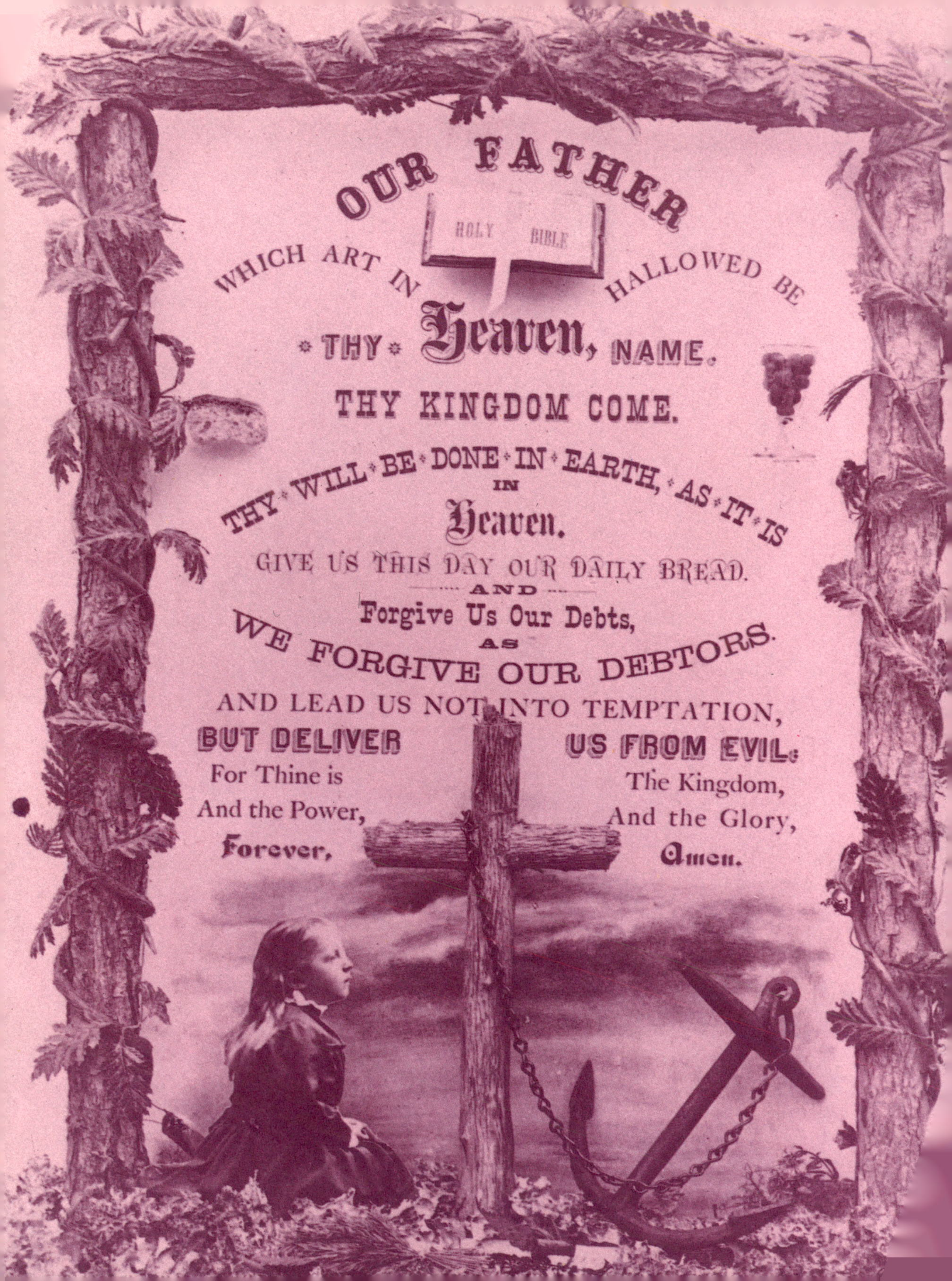

OUR FATHER

HOLY BIBLE

WHICH ART IN · · · HALLOWED BE

* THY * Heaven, NAME.

THY KINGDOM COME.

THY * WILL * BE * DONE * IN * EARTH, * AS * IT * IS

IN

Heaven.

GIVE US THIS DAY OUR DAILY BREAD.

··· AND ···

Forgive Us Our Debts,

AS

WE FORGIVE OUR DEBTORS.

AND LEAD US NOT INTO TEMPTATION,

BUT DELIVER

US FROM EVIL:

For Thine is

The Kingdom,

And the Power,

And the Glory,

Forever,

Amen.

AMEN

AMEN

PRAYERS AND BLESSINGS FROM AROUND THE WORLD

COMPILED BY
SUZANNE SLESIN AND EMILY GWATHMEY
DESIGNED BY STAFFORD CLIFF

PHOTOGRAPHY BY KULBIR THANDI

VIKING
STUDIO
BOOKS

705. – Plougastel-Daoulas – La Procession – Les petits gas du pays portent l'Enfant Jésus

VIKING STUDIO BOOKS
Published by the Penguin Group
Penguin Books USA Inc., 375 Hudson Street,
New York, New York 10014, U.S.A.
Penguin Books Ltd, 27 Wrights Lane,
London W8 5TZ, England
Penguin Books Australia Ltd, Ringwood,
Victoria, Australia
Penguin Books Canada Ltd,
10 Alcorn Avenue,
Toronto, Ontario, Canada M4V 3B2
Penguin Books (N.Z.) Ltd,
182-190 Wairau Road, Auckland 10,
New Zealand

Penguin Books Ltd, Registered Offices:
Harmondsworth, Middlesex, England

First published in 1995 by Viking Penguin,
a division of Penguin Books USA Inc.

1 2 3 4 5 6 7 8 9

ISBN 0-670-86045-X CIP data available

Printed in Singapore.
Set in Copperplate & ITC Century.
Designed by Stafford Cliff.
Production artwork by Matt Sarraf.

ACKNOWLEDGMENTS
We are grateful to the following people for
their support and help with this book:
Doris Leslie Blau
John Taylor Bigelow
Becky Butler and Patty Bralley
Sara Cleary-Burns of The Burns
Collection Ltd.
Jane Creech
Kim Edwards
Rabbi Harold Einsidler
Gail E. Farr of the Balch Institute for
Ethnic Studies
Kim Grant
Charles S. Hirsch
Philip Hughes and Gretchen Andersen at the
Lacquer Chest in London
Nick Kelsh
Kevin Proffitt of the American Jewish Archives
Linda Raymond of the India record office at
the British Museum
Paula Rubenstein
Matt Sarraf
Sheila Schwartz
Alan Scop of Menorah Antiques Ltd.
Jonathan Scott
Jim Shields
Michael Steinberg
Barbara Strauch
Kulbir Thandi

Thank you also to Barbara Hogenson, our
agent, and Michael Fragnito, Barbara Williams,
Marie Timell, Norm Sheinman, Roni Axelrod,
and Cathy Hemming at Penguin USA.

Further credits appear on pages 94-95

AMEN

CONTENTS

INTRODUCTION

PRAYERS FOR FAITH

PRAYERS FOR CHILDREN AND
RITES OF PASSAGE

PRAYERS FOR MARRIAGE

PRAYERS FOR RECOVERY AND
RENEWAL

PRAYERS FOR
PEACE

IN MEMORIAM

INTRODUCTION

In *Amen: Prayers and Blessings from Around the World*, we have tried to gather together some of the best-known and most powerful prayers that have sustained people throughout their lives, prayers that present a universal message of faith, hope and love in a spirit of inclusion and tolerance.

In *Primary Speech*, a book on the psychology of prayer, scholars of religion Ann and Barry Ulanov write, "Everybody prays. People pray whether or not they call it prayer. We pray every time we ask for help, understanding or strength, in or out of religion. Then, who and what we are speak out of us, whether we know it or not. Our movements, our stillness, the expressions on our faces, our tone of voice, our actions, what we dream and daydream, as well as, what we actually put into words say who and what we are."

The godforce to which we pray has been called by a hundred different names: Shiva, Buddha, Jehovah, Allah, Christ, Higher Power, Mother Nature, a sunset, the wind. Yet the intent of all prayer is much the same. We pray for faith and hope, for children and their coming of age, for union and commitment, for renewal and peace and remembrance. These are all universal points in the human journey, points at which we find ourselves desiring and searching for ways to talk to God in the hope of drawing nearer.

But we also have the need to find appropriate and moving words for the situations that arise in a world of increasing diversity and multiculturalism. The pull of wanting to be connected to each other in these difficult modern times has fostered a re-emergence of spirituality. Interfaith marriages as well as same-sex unions suggest a need for prayers and blessings that can both honor individual traditions and serve as ceremonies of celebration and depth of feeling. These are unique and symbolic of our new age.

No matter the culture or country, all important rites of passage in the human journey are marked by prayer. The formalities are as diverse as the world itself. Prayer may be a daily ritual or an occasional act of spontaneity, a song, a poem, a gift of love. We may kneel to worship or fling up our arms in a dance of exaltation. Prayer may be a cry of jubilation at the birth of a child or sorrowful appeal uttered at the death of a loved one. The works and forms of prayer may vary, but the thoughts remain the same. Help me. Forgive me. Increase my strength. Make me wise. Heal me. Inspire me. Restoreth my soul.

Some of our selections – the Lord's Prayer, the 23rd Psalm, the Beatitudes, St. Francis' Humble Plea – are well-known, traditional works of devotion that have been uttered for centuries around the world during times of joy and times of sorrow. Others we have chosen are more contemporary in nature, relating to the metaphysical new age, such as a blessing for a same-sex union or Paramahansa Yogananda's prayer for a United World. The prayers, poems, and blessings have been selected from various religions: Christianity, Hinduism, Judaism, Buddhism, Islam, Confucianism, Shinto and Native American. We believe they acquire new meaning when gathered together and combined with a more modern inclusive view of spirituality.

The need to find an inner pathway to the Spirit is as old as time. "Prayer is the contemplation of the facts of life from the highest point of view," Ralph Waldo Emerson wrote. "It is the soliloquy of a beholding and jubilant soul. It is the Spirit of God pronouncing his works good." A gospel hymn in a fundamentalist church. A prayer chanted at a Tibetan monastery. The sound of "OUM" in solo or group meditation. The call to the Torah. A Native American drumming ceremony. A simple wedding vow. The muezzin calling from the minaret of a mosque. A moment of silence in the glow of a setting sun. The Serenity Prayer spoken in unison at the close of a 12-step meeting.

According to the Dalai Lama, "Every major religion of the world has similar ideals of love, the same goal of benefitting humanity through spiritual practice, and the same effect of making their followers into better human beings." Prayer is a luminous and self-generating kind of energy, a powerful act of honesty and imagination, a rising up and drawing near to God in mind, heart, and spirit, a place where wisdom finds a special dwelling place. Prayer releases an inner power that heals and strengthens. In *Amen*, we offer a pathway to the benefits of prayer in a spirit of peace, openness, and understanding.

Suzanne Slesin, New York.
Emily Gwathmey, Santa Monica.
Stafford Cliff, London.
February, 1995

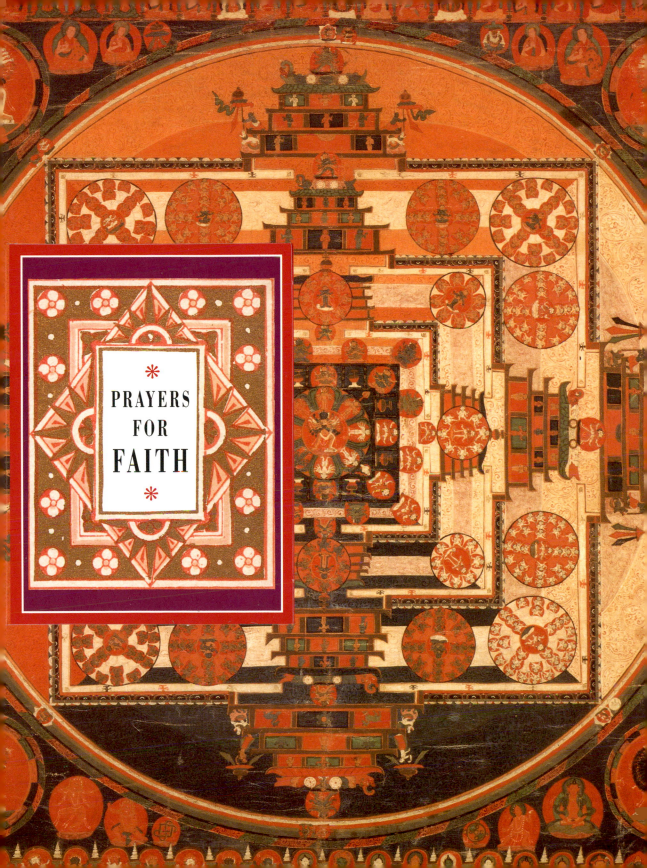

PRAYERS
FOR
FAITH

OUR FATHER
WHO ART IN HEAVEN,
HALLOWED BE THY NAME.
THY KINGDOM COME.
THY WILL BE DONE, ON EARTH
AS IT IS IN HEAVEN.
GIVE US THIS DAY
OUR DAILY BREAD.
AND FORGIVE US OUR DEBTS,
AS WE FORGIVE OUR DEBTORS.
AND LEAD US NOT INTO
TEMPTATION,
BUT DELIVER US FROM EVIL.
FOR THINE IS THE KINGDOM,
AND THE POWER,
AND THE GLORY,
FOR EVER AND EVER.
AMEN.

THE LORD'S PRAYER

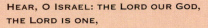

HEAR, O ISRAEL: THE LORD OUR GOD,
THE LORD IS ONE,
AND THOU SHALT LOVE THE LORD THY
GOD WITH ALL THY HEART, AND WITH ALL
THY SOUL, AND WITH ALL THY MIGHT.
AND THESE WORDS, WHICH I COMMAND
THEE THIS DAY,
SHALL BE UPON THY HEART;
AND THOU SHALT TEACH THEM
DILIGENTLY UNTO THY CHILDREN,
AND SHALT TALK OF THEM WHEN THOU
SITTEST IN THY HOUSE,
AND WHEN THOU WALKEST BY THE WAY,
AND WHEN THOU LIEST DOWN,
AND WHEN THOU RISEST UP.
AND THOU SHALT BIND THEM FOR A SIGN
UPON THY HAND, AND THEY SHALL BE
FOR FRONTLETS BETWEEN THINE EYES.
AND THOU SHALT WRITE THEM UPON THE
DOOR POSTS OF THY HOUSE,
AND UPON THY GATES.

SHEMA ISRAEL. OLD TESTAMENT
DEUTORONOMY 6: 4–9

PRAISE BE TO GOD, LORD OF THE WORLDS!
THE COMPASSIONATE, THE MERCIFUL!
KING ON THE DAY OF JUDGMENT!
THEE ONLY DO WE WORSHIP, AND TO THEE
DO WE CRY FOR HELP.
GUIDE THOU US ON THE RIGHT PATH,
THE PATH OF THOSE TO WHOM THOU ART GRACIOUS;
NOT OF THOSE WITH WHOM THOU ART ANGERED,
NOR OF THOSE WHO GO ASTRAY.

THE KORAN: ISLAMIC LORD'S PRAYER

Sunday Evening Service, Half Moon Bay, Thousand Islands, near Gananoque, Ont.

PROTECT ME, O LORD;
MY BOAT IS SO SMALL,
AND YOUR SEA IS SO BIG.

TRADITIONAL CHRISTIAN
FISHERMAN'S PRAYER

LORD, MAKE ME AN INSTRUMENT
OF THY PEACE.
WHERE THERE IS HATRED,
LET ME SOW LOVE.
WHERE THERE IS INJURY, PARDON.
WHERE THERE IS DOUBT, FAITH.
WHERE THERE IS DESPAIR, HOPE.
WHERE THERE IS SADNESS, JOY.

O DIVINE MASTER,
GRANT THAT I MAY NOT SO MUCH SEEK
TO BE CONSOLED, AS TO CONSOLE;
TO BE UNDERSTOOD,
AS TO UNDERSTAND;
TO BE LOVED, AS TO LOVE;
FOR IT IS IN GIVING THAT WE RECEIVE,
IT IS IN PARDONING THAT WE ARE
PARDONED,
AND IT IS IN DYING THAT WE ARE BORN
TO ETERNAL LIFE.

ST. FRANCIS OF ASSISI

OUR EYES MAY SEE SOME UNCLEANNESS,
BUT LET NOT OUR MIND SEE THINGS THAT
ARE NOT CLEAN. OUR EARS MAY HEAR SOME
UNCLEANNESS, BUT LET NOT OUR MIND HEAR
THINGS THAT ARE NOT CLEAN.

SHINTO

GREAT BECOMES THE FRUIT,
GREAT THE ADVANTAGE
OF EARNEST CONTEMPLATION,
WHEN IT IS SET ROUND WITH
UPRIGHT CONDUCT.
GREAT BECOMES THE FRUIT,
GREAT THE ADVANTAGE
OF INTELLECT, WHEN IT IS SET
ROUND WITH EARNEST
CONTEMPLATION.
THE MIND SET ROUND WITH
INTELLIGENCE IS SET QUITE FREE
FROM THE INTOXICATIONS:
FROM THE INTOXICATION
OF SENSUALITY,
FROM THE INTOXICATION
OF BECOMING,
FROM THE INTOXICATION
OF DELUSION,
FROM THE INTOXICATION
OF IGNORANCE.

BUDDHA'S SONG

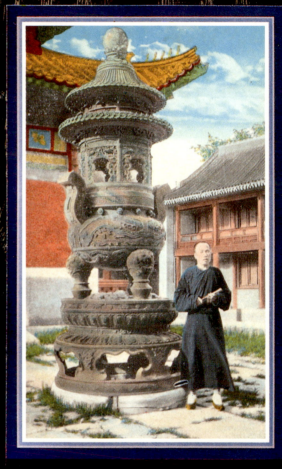

A Happy New Year

זאל צו ניי־יאהר גאט אייך שיקען
טויזענד ברכות, טויזענד גליקען!

PRAYERS
FOR
CHILDREN
AND RITES OF
PASSAGE

✤

SUN, MOON, STARS,
YOU THAT MOVE IN THE HEAVENS,
HEAR THIS MOTHER!
A NEW LIFE HAS COME AMONG YOU.
MAKE ITS PATH SMOOTH THAT IT MAY REACH
THE BROW OF THE FIRST HILL.

WINDS, CLOUDS, RAIN, MIST,
ALL THAT MOVE IN THE AIR,
HEAR THIS MOTHER!
A NEW LIFE HAS COME AMONG YOU.
MAKE ITS PATH SMOOTH THAT IT MAY REACH
THE BROW OF THE SECOND HILL.

HILLS, VALLEYS, RIVERS, LAKES, TREES,
GRASSES,
ALL OF THE EARTH,
HEAR THIS MOTHER!
A NEW LIFE HAS COME AMONG YOU.
MAKE ITS PATH SMOOTH THAT IT MAY REACH
THE BROW OF THE THIRD HILL.

BIRDS THAT FLY IN THE AIR,
ANIMALS THAT DWELL IN THE FOREST,
INSECTS THAT CREEP IN THE GRASSES AND
BURROW IN THE GROUND,
HEAR THIS MOTHER!
A NEW LIFE HAS COME AMONG YOU.
MAKE ITS PATH SMOOTH THAT IT MAY REACH
THE BROW OF THE FOURTH HILL.

ALL THE HEAVENS, AIR AND EARTH,
HEAR THIS MOTHER!
A NEW LIFE HAS COME AMONG YOU.
MAKE ITS PATH SMOOTH—THEN SHALL IT
TRAVEL BEYOND THE FOUR HILLS!

OMAHA TRIBE

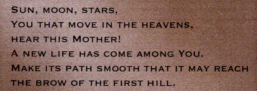

AND YOU, CHILD, WILL BE
CALLED THE PROPHET OF
THE MOST HIGH;
FOR YOU WILL GO BEFORE
THE LORD TO PREPARE
HIS WAYS,
TO GIVE KNOWLEDGE OF
SALVATION TO HIS PEOPLE
IN THE FORGIVENESS OF
THEIR SINS.
THROUGH THE TENDER
MERCY OF OUR GOD,
WHEN THE DAY SHALL
DAWN UPON US FROM
ON HIGH.
TO GIVE LIGHT TO THOSE
WHO SIT IN DARKNESS AND
IN THE SHADOW OF DEATH,
TO GUIDE OUR FEET INTO
THE WAY OF PEACE.

LUKE 1: 76–79

THE HIGHEST GOOD
IS LIKE WATER.
WATER GIVES LIFE TO THE
TEN THOUSAND THINGS
AND DOES NOT STRIVE.
IT FLOWS IN PLACES MEN
REJECT AND SO IS LIKE
THE TAO.
IN DWELLING,
BE CLOSE TO THE LAND.
IN MEDITATION,
GO DEEP IN THE HEART.
IN DEALING WITH OTHERS,
BE GENTLE AND KIND.
IN SPEECH, BE TRUE.
IN RULING, BE JUST.
IN BUSINESS, BE
COMPETENT.
IN ACTION, WATCH THE
TIMING.
NO FIGHT: NO BLAME.

LAO TSE

TO BE ABLE TO PRACTICE
FIVE THINGS EVERYWHERE
UNDER HEAVEN
CONSTITUTES PERFECT
VIRTUE. THEY ARE
GRAVITY, GENEROSITY OF
SOUL, SINCERITY,
EARNESTNESS AND
KINDNESS.

CONFUCIUS

HE WHO BLESSED OUR FATHERS ABRAHAM, ISAAC AND JACOB, MAY
HE BLESS THE BAR MITZVAH BOY AND THE BAT MITZVAH GIRL,
WHO HAVE COME UP TO HONOR GOD AND THE TORAH.
MAY THE HOLY ONE, BLESSED BE HE, PROTECT AND DELIVER HIM
AND HER FROM ALL DISTRESS AND ILLNESS, AND BLESS ALL HER
AND HIS EFFORTS WITH SUCCESS AMONG ALL ISRAEL THEIR
BRETHREN; AND LET US SAY, AMEN.

BAR/BAT MITZVAH

BLESSED ARE YOU, OUR GOD AND THE GOD OF OUR ANCESTORS,
WHO HAS ENABLED US TO FURTHER THE GENERATIONS WITH
COURAGE, AND BLESSED US WITH NEW LIFE.
BLESSED ARE YOU, THE GOD OF LIFE, WHO HAS GIVEN ME
STRENGTH IN THIS DIFFICULT HOUR AND BLESSED ME WITH THE
JOY OF TAKING PART IN THE ACT OF CREATION.
BLESSED ARE YOU, OUR GOD AND THE GOD OF OUR MOTHERS AND
FATHERS, FOR THE MIRACLE OF BIRTH AND THE JOY OF
PARENTHOOD, FOR THE BEAUTY AND LOVE AND THE HARMONY OF
THE LIFE CYCLE.
BLESSED ARE YOU, THE GOD OF LIFE, WHO PROTECTS YOUR
CREATURES AND GIVES THEM WONDROUS CYCLES OF REBIRTH.

RABBI ELYSE GOLDSTEIN

GOD SPAKE THESE WORDS, AND SAID:
I AM THE LORD THY GOD; THOU SHALT
HAVE NONE OTHER GODS BUT ME.

THOU SHALT NOT MAKE TO THYSELF
ANY GRAVEN IMAGE, NOR THE
LIKENESS OF ANY THING THAT IS IN
HEAVEN ABOVE, OR IN THE EARTH
BENEATH, OR IN THE WATER UNDER
THE EARTH; THOU SHALT NOT BOW
DOWN TO THEM, NOR WORSHIP THEM.

THOU SHALT NOT TAKE THE NAME OF
THE LORD THY GOD IN VAIN.

REMEMBER THAT THOU KEEP HOLY THE
SABBATH-DAY.

HONOR THY FATHER AND THY MOTHER.

THOU SHALT DO NO MURDER.

THOU SHALT NOT COMMIT ADULTERY.

THOU SHALT NOT STEAL.

THOU SHALT NOT BEAR FALSE
WITNESS AGAINST THY NEIGHBOR.

THOU SHALT NOT COVET.

LORD HAVE MERCY UPON US, AND
WRITE ALL THESE THY LAWS IN OUR
HEARTS, WE BESEECH THEE.

HOLY COMMUNION DECALOGUE
FROM THE BOOK OF COMMON PRAYER

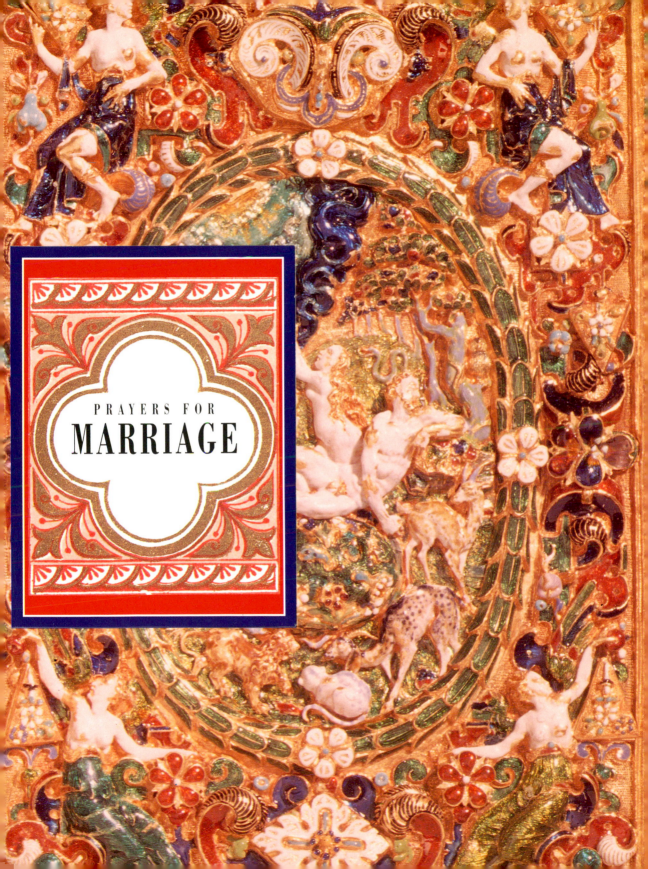

PRAYERS FOR
MARRIAGE

FROM THE BEGINNING OF CREATION
GOD MADE THEM MALE AND FEMALE.

THIS IS WHY A MAN MUST LEAVE
FATHER AND MOTHER, AND THE TWO
BECOME ONE BODY.
THEY ARE NO LONGER TWO,
THEREFORE, BUT ONE BODY.

SO THEN, WHAT GOD HAS UNITED,
MAN MUST NOT DIVIDE.

THIS IS THE GOSPEL OF THE LORD.

MARK 10: 6–9

THIS IS MY COMMITMENT IN YOU:
TO ALWAYS BE HERE FOR YOU,
IN COMFORT AND IN JOY FOR GOOD, FOR BETTER,
AND FOR BEST; TO ALWAYS VALUE YOUR THOUGHTS
AND FEELINGS, EVEN WHEN THEY MAY DIFFER FROM
MY OWN; TO ALWAYS BE HONEST WITH YOU,
EVEN WHEN THAT HONESTY MAY BE HURTFUL;
TO ALWAYS RESPECT YOU AS MY BEST FRIEND,
MY ONE AND ONLY LOVE, AND MY SOUL MATE,
IN THIS LIFE AND HEREAFTER;
AND TO NEVER LET ANY MAN, WOMAN, ANIMAL,
OR OBJECT BECOME MORE IMPORTANT TO ME
THAN THIS, OUR MUTUAL BOND.

SAME-SEX WEDDING

O LORD OUR GOD, WHO GRANT US WHAT WE ASK FOR
OUR SALVATION, WHO HATH COMMANDED US TO LOVE
EACH OTHER AND TO PARDON EACH OTHER OUR
TRANSGRESSIONS, BLESS, LORD, GIVER OF GOOD
THINGS, LOVER OF MANKIND, THESE TWO SERVANTS
OF THINE WHO LOVE EACH OTHER WITH A LOVE OF
THE SPIRIT AND HAVE COME TO THY HOLY TEMPLE
WISHING TO RECEIVE THY SANCTIFICATION AND
BENEDICTION; GRANT THEM UNABASHED
FAITHFULNESS AND SINCERE LOVE, AND JUST AS YOU
GAVE THY HOLY DISCIPLES AND APOSTLES THY PEACE
AND LOVE, GRANT THEM ALSO TO THESE, CHRIST OUR
GOD, GIVING THEM ALL THESE THINGS NECESSARY
FOR SALVATION AND ETERNAL LIFE.

11TH–12TH CENTURY

LET THE EARTH OF MY BODY BE
MIXED WITH THE EARTH MY
BELOVED WALKS ON.
LET THE FIRE OF MY BODY
BE THE BRIGHTNESS IN THE
MIRROR THAT REFLECTS
HIS FACE.
LET THE WATER OF MY BODY
JOIN THE WATERS OF THE LOTUS
POOL HE BATHES IN.
LET THE BREATH OF MY
BODY BE AIR LAPPING
HIS TIRED LIMBS.
LET ME BE SKY, AND MOVING
THROUGH ME THAT
CLOUD-DARK SHYAMA,
MY BELOVED.

HINDU LOVE POEM

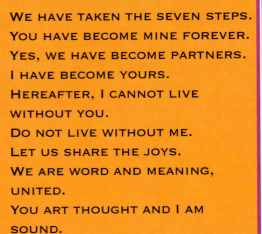

WE HAVE TAKEN THE SEVEN STEPS.
YOU HAVE BECOME MINE FOREVER.
YES, WE HAVE BECOME PARTNERS.
I HAVE BECOME YOURS.
HEREAFTER, I CANNOT LIVE
WITHOUT YOU.
DO NOT LIVE WITHOUT ME.
LET US SHARE THE JOYS.
WE ARE WORD AND MEANING,
UNITED.
YOU ART THOUGHT AND I AM
SOUND.
MAY THE NIGHTS BE HONEY-SWEET
FOR US; MAY THE MORNINGS BE
HONEY-SWEET FOR US; MAY THE
EARTH BE HONEY-SWEET FOR US;
MAY THE HEAVENS BE HONEY-
SWEET FOR US.
MAY THE PLANTS BE HONEY-SWEET
FOR US; MAY THE SUN BE ALL
HONEY FOR US; MAY THE COWS
YIELD US HONEY-SWEET MILK!
AS THE HEAVENS ARE STABLE, AS
THE EARTH IS STABLE, AS THE
MOUNTAINS ARE STABLE, AS THE
WHOLE UNIVERSE IS STABLE,
SO MAY OUR UNION BE
PERMANENTLY SETTLED.

HINDU: THE SEVEN STEPS

THE VOICE OF MY BELOVED!
BEHOLD, HE COMES, LEAPING UPON THE
MOUNTAINS, BOUNDING OVER THE HILLS.
MY BELOVED IS LIKE A GAZELLE,
OR A YOUNG STAG.
BEHOLD, THERE HE STANDS BEHIND OUR
WALL, GAZING IN AT THE WINDOWS,
LOOKING THROUGH THE LATTICE.
MY BELOVED SPEAKS AND SAYS TO ME:
ARISE, MY LOVE, MY FAIR ONE, AND COME
AWAY; FOR LO, THE WINTER IS PAST,
THE RAIN IS OVER AND GONE.
THE FLOWERS APPEAR ON THE EARTH,
THE TIME OF SINGING HAS COME,
AND THE VOICE OF THE TURTLEDOVE
IS HEARD IN OUR LAND.
THE FIG TREE PUTS FORTH ITS FIGS,
AND THE VINES ARE IN BLOSSOM;
THEY GIVE FORTH FRAGRANCE.
ARISE, MY LOVE, MY FAIR ONE,
AND COME AWAY.

SONG OF SOLOMON: 2: 8–13

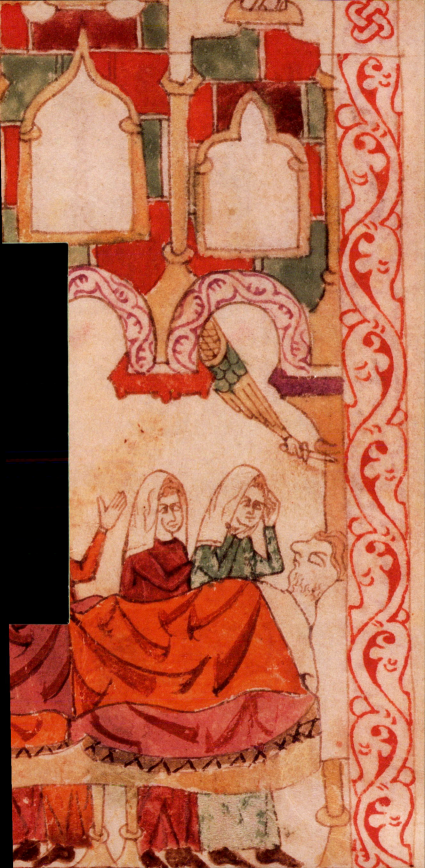

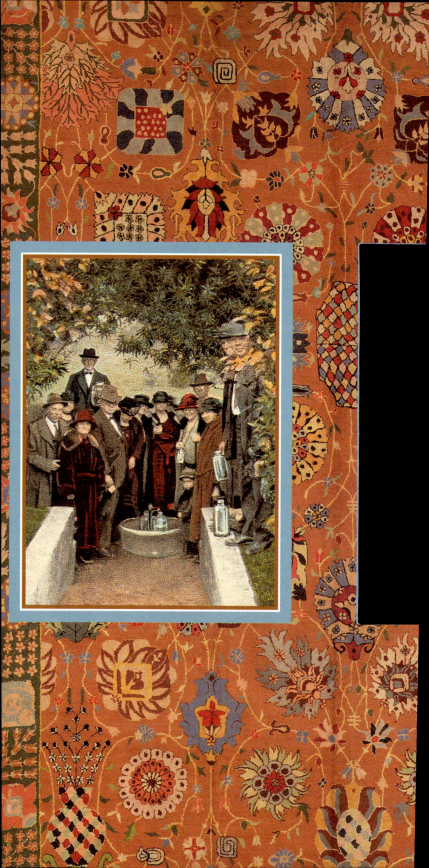

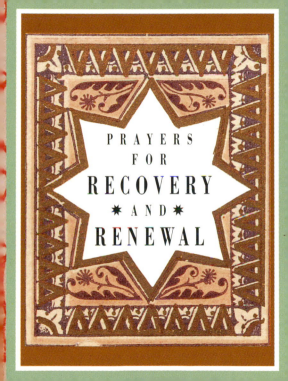

PRAYERS
FOR
RECOVERY
✱ AND ✱
RENEWAL

LORD, OPEN OUR EYES,
THAT WE MAY SEE YOU IN OUR
BROTHERS AND SISTERS.
LORD, OPEN OUR EARS,
THAT WE MAY HEAR THE CRIES
OF THE HUNGRY,
THE COLD,
THE FRIGHTENED,
THE OPPRESSED.
LORD, OPEN OUR HEARTS,
THAT WE MAY LOVE EACH OTHER
AS YOU LOVE US.
RENEW IN US YOUR SPIRIT
LORD, FREE US AND
MAKE US ONE.

MOTHER TERESA

GOD, GRANT ME THE SERENITY
TO ACCEPT THE THINGS I
CANNOT CHANGE.
THE COURAGE TO CHANGE THE
THINGS I CAN.
AND THE WISDOM TO KNOW
THE DIFFERENCE.
GRANT ME PATIENCE WITH THE
THINGS THAT TAKE TIME.
TOLERANCE OF THE STRUGGLES
OF OTHERS THAT MAY BE
DIFFERENT FROM MY OWN.
APPRECIATION FOR ALL I HAVE
AND THE WILLINGNESS TO
GET UP AND TRY AGAIN.
ONE DAY AT A TIME.

THE SERENITY PRAYER

AND THEN ALL THAT HAS DIVIDED US
WILL MERGE

AND THEN COMPASSION WILL
BE WEDDED TO POWER

AND THEN SOFTNESS WILL COME TO A
WORLD THAT IS HARSH AND UNKIND

AND THEN BOTH MEN AND WOMEN
WILL BE GENTLE

AND THEN BOTH WOMEN AND MEN
WILL BE STRONG

AND THEN NO PERSON WILL
BE SUBJECT TO ANOTHER'S WILL

AND THEN ALL WILL BE RICH
AND FREE AND VARIED

AND THEN THE GREED OF SOME
WILL GIVE WAY TO THE NEEDS OF MANY

AND THEN ALL WILL SHARE
EQUALLY IN THE EARTH'S ABUNDANCE

AND THEN ALL WILL CARE FOR
THE SICK AND THE WEAK AND THE OLD

AND THEN ALL WILL NOURISH THE YOUNG

AND THEN ALL WILL CHERISH
LIFE'S CREATURES

AND THEN ALL WILL LIVE IN HARMONY
WITH EACH OTHER AND THE EARTH

AND THEN EVERYWHERE WILL BE
CALLED EDEN ONCE AGAIN.

JUDY CHICAGO

LIFE THE WORLDWIDE KINGDOM OF FRIENDLY CITIZENS

UMMERLAND BEACH OHIO.

PRECIOUS LORD, TAKE MY HAND,
LEAD ME ON, LET ME STAND,
I AM TIRED, I AM WEAK, I AM WORN;
THRU THE STORM, THRU THE NIGHT,
LEAD ME TO THE LIGHT,
TAKE MY HAND, PRECIOUS LORD,
LEAD ME HOME.

WHEN MY WAY GROWS DREAR, PRECIOUS
LORD, LINGER NEAR,
WHEN MY LIFE IS ALMOST GONE,
HEAR MY CRY, HEAR MY CALL,
HOLD MY HAND LEST I FALL;
TAKE MY HAND, PRECIOUS LORD,
LEAD ME HOME.

WHEN THE DARKNESS APPEARS AND THE
NIGHT DRAWS NEAR,
AND THE DAY IS PAST AND GONE,
AT THE RIVER I STAND,
GUIDE MY FEET, HOLD MY HAND;
TAKE MY HAND, PRECIOUS LORD,
LEAD ME HOME.

BAPTISM

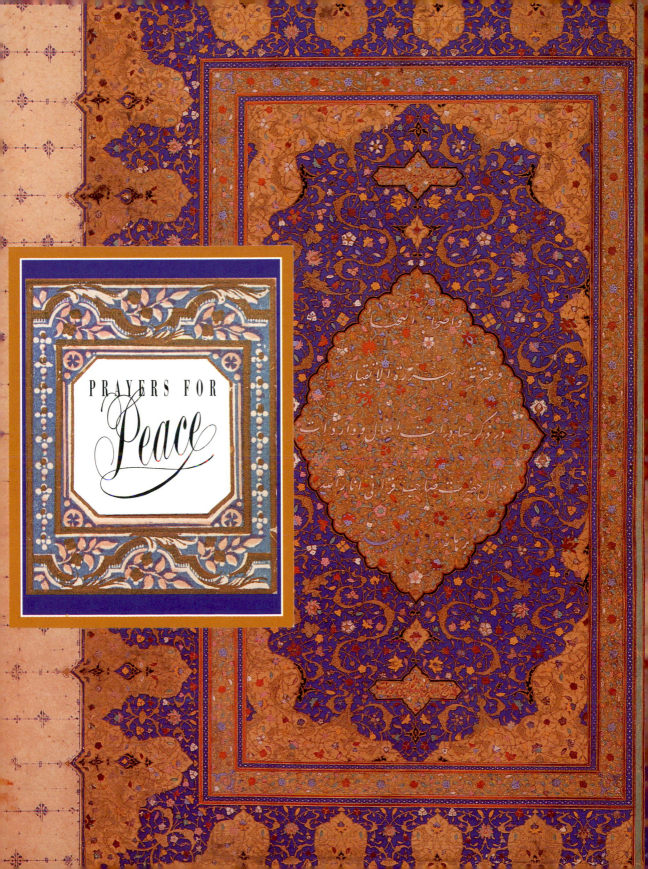

PRAYERS FOR
Peace

MAY THE HEADS OF ALL COUNTRIES AND
RACES BE GUIDED TO UNDERSTAND THAT
MEN OF ALL NATIONS ARE PHYSICALLY
AND SPIRITUALLY ONE: PHYSICALLY ONE,
BECAUSE WE ARE THE DESCENDANTS OF
COMMON PARENTS — THE SYMBOLIC ADAM
AND EVE; AND SPIRITUALLY ONE,
BECAUSE WE ARE THE IMMORTAL
CHILDREN OF OUR FATHER, BOUND BY
ETERNAL LINKS OF BROTHERHOOD.

LET US PRAY IN OUR HEARTS FOR A
LEAGUE OF SOULS AND A UNITED WORLD.
THOUGH WE MAY SEEM DIVIDED BY RACE,
CREED, COLOR, CLASS, AND POLITICAL
PREJUDICES, STILL, AS CHILDREN OF THE
ONE GOD WE ARE ABLE IN OUR SOULS TO
FEEL BROTHERHOOD AND WORLD UNITY.
MAY WE WORK FOR THE CREATION OF A
UNITED WORLD IN WHICH EVERY NATION
WILL BE A USEFUL PART, GUIDED BY GOD
THROUGH MAN'S ENLIGHTENED
CONSCIENCE.

IN OUR HEARTS WE CAN ALL LEARN TO BE
FREE FROM HATE AND SELFISHNESS.
LET US PRAY FOR HARMONY AMONG THE
NATIONS, THAT THEY MARCH HAND IN
HAND THROUGH THE GATE OF A FAIR NEW
CIVILIZATION.
PARAMAHANSA YOGANANDA

Raja Yoga Orchestra, In

International Theosophical Headquarters,
Point Loma California

THIS WE KNOW, ALL THINGS ARE CONNECTED,
LIKE THE BLOOD WHICH UNITES ONE FAMILY.
ALL THINGS ARE CONNECTED. WHATEVER BEFALLS THE
EARTH, BEFALLS THE SONS OF THE EARTH.
MAN DID NOT WEAVE THE WEB OF LIFE; HE IS MERELY A
STRAND IN IT. WHATEVER HE DOES TO THE WEB,
HE DOES TO HIMSELF.

CHIEF SEATTLE OF THE DWAMISH TRIBE

WEAVE FOR US A GARMENT OF BRIGHTNESS;
MAY THE WARP BE THE WHITE LIGHT OF MORNING,
MAY THE WEFT BE THE RED LIGHT OF EVENING,
MAY THE FRINGES BE THE FALLING RAIN,
MAY THE BORDER BE THE STANDING RAINBOW.
THUS WEAVE FOR US A GARMENT OF BRIGHTNESS,
THAT WE MAY WALK FITTINGLY WHERE BIRDS SING,
THAT WE MAY WALK FITTINGLY WHERE GRASS IS GREEN,
O OUR MOTHER THE EARTH, O OUR FATHER THE SKY.

NATIVE AMERICAN

THE WOLF SHALL DWELL WITH THE LAMB,
AND THE LEOPARD SHALL LIE DOWN WITH THE KID,
AND THE CALF AND THE YOUNG LION AND THE FATLING TOGETHER,
AND A LITTLE CHILD SHALL LEAD THEM.

THE COW AND THE BEAR SHALL FEED;
THEIR YOUNG ONES SHALL LIE DOWN TOGETHER;
AND THE LION SHALL EAT STRAW LIKE THE OX.

THE SUCKING CHILD SHALL PLAY OVER THE HOLE OF THE ASP,
AND THE WEANED CHILD SHALL PUT HIS HAND ON THE ADDER'S DEN.
THEY SHALL NOT HURT OR DESTROY IN ALL MY HOLY MOUNTAIN;
FOR THE EARTH SHALL BE FULL OF THE KNOWLEDGE OF THE LORD AS THE
WATERS COVER THE SEA.

ISAIAH 11: 6–9

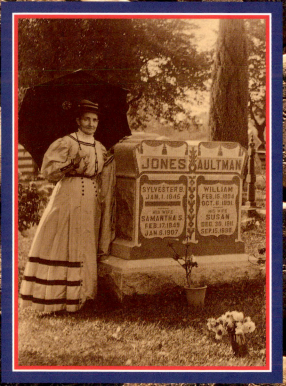

JONES AULTMAN

SYLVESTER B.
JAN. 1, 1845
WILLIAM
FEB. 15, 1804
OCT. 6, 1891.

HIS WIFE
SAMANTHA S.
FEB. 17, 1849
JAN. 6, 1907
HIS WIFE
SUSAN
DEC. 30, 1811
SEP. 15, 1899

TO
LIVE IN HEARTS
WE LEAVE
BEHIND IS NOT
TO DIE.

FROM THE UNREAL LEAD ME TO THE REAL;
FROM DARKNESS LEAD ME TO LIGHT;
FROM DEATH LEAD ME TO DEATHLESSNESS.

HINDU

O THOU SHINING ONE,
THOU KNOWEST ALL OUR WAYS.
WE UTTER PRAISE OF THEE!
THOU ART WOMAN, THOU ART MAN;
THOU ART YOUTH, THOU ART MAIDEN . . .
THOU ART THE DARK BLUE BEE,
THOU ART THE GREEN PARROT WITH RED EYES,
THOU ART THE THUNDER-CLOUD,
THE SEASONS, THE SEAS.
THOU ART OUR FATHER. THOU ART OUR MOTHER.
THOU ART OUR BELOVED FRIEND.

HINDU

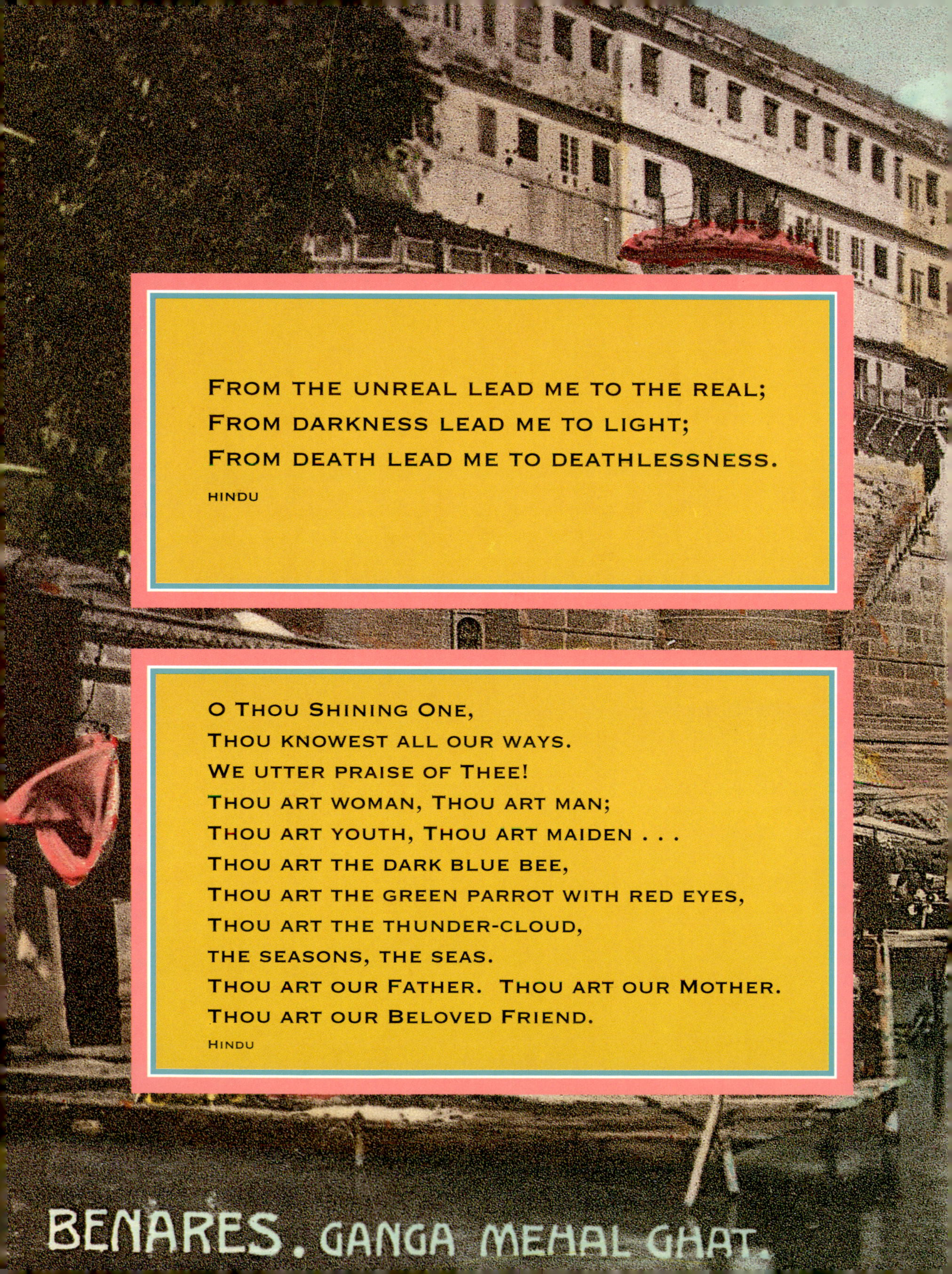

BENARES. GANGA MEHAL GHAT.

EXTOLLED AND HALLOWED BE THE
NAME OF GOD THROUGHOUT THE
WORLD WHICH HE HAS CREATED,
AND WHICH HE GOVERNS ACCORDING
TO HIS RIGHTEOUS WILL. JUST IS
HE IN ALL HIS WAYS, AND WISE ARE
ALL HIS DECREES. MAY HIS
KINGDOM COME AND HIS WILL BE
DONE IN ALL THE EARTH.

PRAISED BE THE LORD OF LIFE, THE
RIGHTEOUS JUDGE, FOR EVER MORE.
WHATSOEVER PRAISE WE WOULD
RENDER UNTO GOD, HOWSOEVER
WE WOULD ADORE THE MOST HIGH,
WE WOULD YET FAIL TO GIVE HIM
THE GLORY DUE TO HIS GREAT NAME.
EVEN IN THE HOUR OF BEREAVEMENT
AND SORROW, WE FEEL THE MAJESTY
OF GOD AND WILL GIVE THANKS, FOR
HIS MANIFOLD MERCIES.

MAY THE FATHER OF PEACE SEND
PEACE TO ALL WHO MOURN AND
COMFORT ALL THE BEREAVED AMONG
US. AMEN.

JEWISH: MOURNER'S KADDISH

John Brown's Grave, Adirondack Mts., N. Y

THE LORD IS MY SHEPHERD;
I SHALL NOT WANT.
HE MAKETH ME TO LIE DOWN IN GREEN PASTURES;
HE LEADETH ME BESIDE THE STILL WATERS.
HE RESTORETH MY SOUL;
HE LEADETH ME IN THE PATHS OF RIGHTEOUSNESS FOR HIS NAME'S SAKE.
YEA, THOUGH I WALK THROUGH THE VALLEY OF THE SHADOW OF DEATH,
I WILL FEAR NO EVIL, FOR THOU ART WITH ME; THY ROD AND THY STAFF
THEY COMFORT ME.
THOU PREPAREST A TABLE BEFORE ME IN THE PRESENCE OF MINE ENEMIES;
THOU ANOINTEST MY HEAD WITH OIL, MY CUP RUNNETH OVER.
SURELY GOODNESS AND MERCY SHALL FOLLOW ME ALL THE DAYS OF MY
LIFE; AND I SHALL DWELL IN THE HOUSE OF THE LORD FOREVER.

OLD TESTAMENT: THE 23RD PSALM

REMEMBER THY LORD
WITHIN THYSELF
HUMBLY AND WITH AWE,
BELOW THY BREATH,
AT MORN AND EVENING.
AND IN THE NIGHTTIME,
ALSO HYMN HIS PRAISE
AT THE SETTING OF THE
STARS.
THE KORAN

For everything there is a season,
and a time for every matter under heaven:
A time to be born, and a time to die;
A time to plant, and a time to pluck up what is planted;
A time to kill, and a time to heal;
A time to break down, and a time to build up;
A time to weep, and a time to laugh;
A time to mourn, and a time to dance;
A time to cast away stones, and a time to gather stones together;
A time to embrace, and a time to refrain from embracing;
A time to seek, and a time to lose;
A time to keep, and a time to cast away;
A time to rend, and a time to sew;
A time to keep silence, and a time to speak;
A time to love, and a time to hate;
A time for war, and a time for peace.

ECCLESIASTES 3

So live that when the summons comes
To join the innumerable caravan
Which moves to that mysterious realm
Where each shall take his chamber
In the silent halls of death
Thou go not like the quarry slave of night
Scourged to his dungeon
But sustained and soothed by an unfaltering
Trust. Approach thy grave like one
Who wraps the drapery of his couch about him
And lies down to pleasant dreams.

WILLIAM CULLEN BRYANT

BLESSED ARE THE POOR IN SPIRIT: FOR THEIRS IS THE KINGDOM OF HEAVEN.
BLESSED ARE THEY THAT MOURN: FOR THEY SHALL BE COMFORTED.
BLESSED ARE THE MEEK: FOR THEY SHALL INHERIT THE EARTH.
BLESSED ARE THEY WHICH DO HUNGER AND THIRST AFTER RIGHTEOUSNESS:
FOR THEY SHALL BE FILLED.
BLESSED ARE THE MERCIFUL: FOR THEY SHALL OBTAIN MERCY.
BLESSED ARE THE PURE IN HEART: FOR THEY SHALL SEE GOD.
BLESSED ARE THE PEACEMAKERS: FOR THEY SHALL BE CALLED THE
CHILDREN OF GOD.
BLESSED ARE THEY WHICH ARE PERSECUTED FOR RIGHTEOUSNESS SAKE:
FOR THEIRS IS THE KINGDOM OF HEAVEN.

THE BEATITUDES—MATTHEW 5: 3–12

WE WISH TO THANK the following individuals, libraries, institutions and publishers for the use of the photographs, illustrations, and texts:

Cover: Graduation circle, Westover School, Middlebury, CT, photograph by Nick Kelsh.
End papers: Pilgrims on the way to Lourdes, France, private collection.
Opposite half title: Turn of the century Lord's Prayer, private collection.
Half title page: Postcard, Chinese Sunday school children, private collection.
Opposite title page: Young children in prayer, France, circa 1910, Collection Roger-Viollet.
Copyright page: Postcard, Religious procession, France, private collection.
Introduction: Postcard, Muslim pilgrims, private collection.
Postcard, Easter sunrise service, Junipero Serra's Memorial Cross, Riverside, CA. private collection.

PRAYERS FOR FAITH:
Cosmati pavement, Westminster Abbey, courtesy of the Dean and Chapter of Westminster, London.
Inset: Postcard, Church of the Holy Sepulcher, Jerusalem, private collection.
Kalachakra Mandala, Central Tibet, late sixteenth century, photograph © 1991 John Bigelow Taylor, from the collection of the Musée Guimet, Paris.
Architectural drawing, Church window detail, private collection.
Inset: Postcard, The Holy Stairs, Church of Saint Anne de Beaupré, Quebec, private collection.
Children in prayer, France, Collection Roger-Viollet.
Postcard, The Wailing Wall, Jerusalem, private collection.
Inset: Postcard, The reading of the Koran, private collection.
Postcard photograph, circa 1910, France, private collection.
Postcard, Sunday evening service, Ontario, Canada, private collection.
Children at prayer, photograph by Laure Albin Guillot, France, Collection Roger-Viollet.

Peace.

HE Lord bless thee and keep thee; The Lord make His face to shine upon thee and be gracious unto thee; The Lord lift up his countenance upon thee and give thee peace.

Copyrighted 1907. D. HILLSON.

CREDITS

Text: Shinto prayer from *God of a Hundred Names* by Barbara Greene and Victor Gollancz, Victor Gollancz, Shinto priest with gohei, private collection.
Shinto priest, private collection.
Text: "Buddha's Song" from *The Minor Anthology of the Pali Canon Part II*, copyright The Pali Text Society, Oxford, England.
Postcard, Lama priest and incense burner, Peking, China, private collection.
Postcard, Buddha, Kobe, Japan, private collection.

PRAYERS FOR CHILDREN AND RITES OF PASSAGE:
Postcard, Interior of Jewish synagogue, Newport, RI, private collection.
Inset: Postcard, Jewish New Year, private collection.
Virgin and Child, *The Book of Kells*, courtesy of The Board of Trinity College Dublin, Ireland.
Text: bedtime prayer adapted by

Miriam Drury from *Prayers for Children*, a Golden Book, Western Publishing Co., New York, 1952.
Hebrew illustration, The Oriental and India Office Collections, by permission of The British Library, London, England.
Inset: Christening photograph, circa 1900, private collection.
Class photograph, New York, NY, 1952-53, private collection.
Ida Palmer Walulutuna and baby, photograph by Joseph K. Dixon, neg. no. 317180, courtesy of Department of Library Services, American Museum of Natural History, New York, NY.
Festival in honor of Joan of Arc, June 8, 1913, Campiegne, France, Collection Roger-Viollet.
Postcard photograph, graduation day, March 21, 1929, American, private collection.
Graduation photograph of Benjamin and Minnie Margolin, circa 1914, New York, NY, private collection.
Text: "Eight" from *Tao Te Ching* by Lao Tsu, translated by Gia-Fu Feng and Jane English. Copyright © 1972 by Gia-Fu Feng and Jane English, Reprinted by permission of Alfred Knopf, Inc.
Jason Douglas Loh, a Chinese-American at his "Full Month" party, New York, NY, 1986, photograph by Douglas Loh, courtesy the Balch Institute for Ethnic Studies, Philadelphia, PA.
Graduation circle, Westover School, Middlebury, CN, photograph by Nick Kelsh.
Text: reprinted from *Covenant of the Heart: Prayers, Poems and Meditations from the Women of Reform Judaism*, copyright © 1993, National Federation of Temple Sisterhoods, used by permission of Rabbi Elyse Goldstein.
Bat-Mitzvah of Wisberg triplets, Pittsfield, MA, American Jewish Archives, Cincinnati Campus, Hebrew Union College Jewish Institute of Religion.
Postcard photograph, Bar-Mitzvah boy, American, 1910-20, Menorah Antiques Ltd., Brooklyn, NY.
Communion portraits, France and United States, private collection.

PRAYERS FOR MARRIAGE:
Baroque church interior, Puebla Tonantzintla, Mexico, Robert Frerck/Odyssey/Chicago, © Robert Harding Picture Library.
Inset: Anonymous wedding portrait, American, private collection.
Book cover, Adam and Eve, 1815, courtesy of the Board of Trustees of the Victoria and Albert Museum, London, England.
Hearts quilt, courtesy Thos. K. Woodard American Quilts and Antiques, New York, NY.
Inset: Bridal favor badge, American, private collection.
Wedding photograph of Frank and Connie Sabin, London, 1934, private collection.
Wedding photograph, private collection.
Bridal procession 1904, France, Collection Roger-Viollet.
Text: "The Vows from David to Norman" from *The Essential Guide to Lesbian and Gay Weddings* by Tess Ayers and Paul Brown. Copyright © 1994 Tess Ayers and Paul Brown. Reprinted by permission of HarperCollins Publishers.
Patty Bralley and Becky Butler, photograph by Lucy Phenix. Courtesy Patty Bralley and Becky Butler.
Photograph by F. Bazin, France, 1869, private collection.
Text: Hindu love poem from *In Praise of Krishna* by Edward Dimock and Denise Levertov. Copyright © 1967, The Asia Society, Inc. Used by permission of Doubleday, a division of Bantam Doubleday Dell Publishing Group, Inc.
Postcard photograph, Hindu marriage, private collection.
Jewish wedding at Victoria Street, London, 1928, courtesy of the Hulton Deutsch Collection Limited, London, England.

PRAYERS FOR RECOVERY AND RENEWAL:
The nave at Bourges Cathedral, France, photograph © Michael Holford.
Inset: Postcard, Basilica of the Virgin, Lourdes, France, private collection.

Hebrew manuscript, The Oriental and India Office Collections, by permission of The British Library, London, England.
Early 20th century Oriental hooked carpet, courtesy of Doris Leslie Blau Gallery, Inc., New York, NY.
Inset: Postcard, Tourists at the Fountain of Youth, St. Petersburg, FL, 1926, private collection.
Text: prayer by Mother Teresa.
Postcard, Fatima, Lisbon, Portugal, private collection.
Panoramic photograph of group of pilgrims at Lourdes, France, private collection.
Hands, photograph Mark Haven, New York, NY.
Postcard photograph of YWCA girls camp, Summerland Beach, Ohio, private collection.
Text: "Merger Poem" from *The Dinner Party* by Judy Chicago, copyright © Judy Chicago, 1979.
Postcard, Baptism near Norfolk, VA, 1925, private collection.

PRAYERS FOR PEACE:
Attarine Medressu, Fez el Bali, Morocco photograph by David Beatty, © Robert Harding Picture Library.
Inset: Postcard, Muslim call to prayer, India, private collection.
Islamic manuscript, The Oriental and India Office Collections, by permission of The British Library, London, England.
Moorish tile design, courtesy of the Board of Trustees of the Victoria and Albert Museum, London, England.
Inset: Postcard, Muslim prayers, Turkey, private collection.
Postcard photograph, North African family, private collection.
Text: "Prayer for a United World" from *Metaphysical Meditations* by Paramahansa Yogananda published by Self-Realization Fellowship, Los Angeles, U.S.A.
Postcard, Raja Yoga Orchestra, Point Loma, CA. circa 1910, private collection.
Text: "Weave for Us" from *American Indian Prose and Poetry* by Margot Astrov, Copyright © 1946 by Margot Astrov. Copyright renewed. Reprinted by permission of

HarperCollins Publishers, Inc.
Native American group at Little Billy's camp, Florida 1910, photograph by Julian A. Dimock, neg. no. 48158, courtesy of the Department of Library Services, American Museum of Natural History, New York, NY.
Blackfoot travois, photograph by Joseph K. Dixon, neg. no. 316642, courtesy of the Department of Library Services, American Museum of Natural History, New York, NY.
Stereoscopic photograph of Canadian nuns by L. P. Vallee, private collection.

IN MEMORIAM:
Marrakech Saadian tombs, Morocco, photograph by Adam Woolfitt, © Robert Harding Picture Library.
Inset: Postcard photograph, American, private collection.
Manuscript letter M, courtesy of the Board of Trustees of the Victoria and Albert Museum, London, England.
Ancient carved prayer stones at Ladakh, India, photograph by David Brittain.
Inset: Postcard photograph, American, circa 1900, private collection.
Sweeper at French cemetery, 1941, France, Collection Roger-Viollet.
Postcard photograph, the Ganges at Benares, India, private collection.
Jewish orthodox funeral, Israel, circa 1950, courtesy Stanley B. Burns, M.D. and The Burns Archive.
Postcard, John Brown's grave, Adirondack Mountains, NY, private collection.
Moslem funeral convoy, Tlemcen, Morocco, Collection Roger-Viollet.
Victorian memorial wreath, photograph by C.A. Howe, Ware, MA, private collection.
Graveside service, photograph by J. Trzpis, Amsterdam, NY, private collection.

Credits page: Postcard, 1913, New York, NY, private collection.
Postcard, Interior of the mosque el-Djedid, Algiers, private collection.